EVALUATION

10 Significant Ways for Measuring and Improving Training Impact

SANDRA MERWIN
Introduction by BOB PIKE

Jossey-Bass Pfeiffer
San Francisco

Creative Training Techniques Press

ISBN: 0-7879-5123-4

Printed in the United States of America

Published by

JOSSEY-BASS/PFEIFFER
A Wiley Company
350 Sansome St.
San Francisco, CA 94104-1342
415.433.1740; Fax 415.433.0499
800.274.4434; Fax 800.569.0443

www.pfeiffer.com

Creative Training Techniques Press
7620 West 78th Street
Minneapolis, MN 55439
(800) 383-9210(612) 829-1954;
Fax (612) 829-0260

Visit our website at:
http://www.cttbobpike.com

Printing 10 9 8 7 6 5 4 3 2

This book is printed on acid-free, recycled stock that meets or exceeds the minimum GPO and EPA requirements for recycled paper.

EVALUATION:
Ten Significant Ways for Measuring & Improving Training Impact

Table of Contents

Acknowledgement

My sincere appreciation

and thanks to

R. Dennis Cook, Ph.D.,

the statistical consultant.

An Introduction by Robert W. Pike, CSP

Welcome to the wonderful world of evaluation! Wonderful? Yes, wonderful! Wonderful and exciting! Evaluation is the part of the training process that enables us to see that we have achieved results - that the training we've so painstakingly designed and delivered has made a difference to our participants and the organization.

And that's the goal of evaluation - to measure current results and to improve future results.

Now, just what is evaluation? Let's start to answer that question by looking at what it's not. Evaluation is not:

- Data for data's sake.

  We don't collect information just to have it. We do it because evaluation makes a contribution to improving the impact and value of training.
- Punitive.

  Evaluation is done to measure and improve the effectiveness of training, not to reward those who achieve and punish those who do not. Evaluation is part of a norm that says everyone can achieve. If some do not, then we improve the training process, participant selection criteria, etc. so that more people succeed the next time.
- Egocentric.

  Evaluation is not done to massage anyone's ego. It's not an opportunity for the trainer to hear one more time how wonderful the program (and of course the trainer!) was. It is done because evaluation can help prove the present value of training and increase the future value of the program. Evaluation data is used to improve training.

- Smile sheets.

  Whether or not people liked the program is a very, very small part of evaluation. And if that's the only thing we're looking at, then we're not really doing evaluation. The focus of evaluation is to help improve the results our training achieves, not simply prove how happy people were with the program or the instructor.

- One time.

  Our organizations, people, economy and environments are not static; evaluation cannot be either. We must continually be measuring the effectiveness of what we do so that as changes occur we can make adjustments to continually maintain peak performance of our programs and their results.

- Complex.

  Effective evaluation does not have to be complex. Simple tests and measurements can be used to give a very clear picture of the effectiveness of our training.

- The realm of scientists and statisticians.

  Evaluation is meant to be a tool to improve results over time, not a full employment strategy for those with a Ph.D. in math or statistics. The methods in this book were designed to be effective for average people who want to improve the effectiveness of their training.

For evaluation to be effective, however, there are some assumptions that we're making from the beginning of this book - and some prerequisites. First the assumptions: at the very least we're assuming two things are true for any training program. The first is that your evaluation system is in place before the program is conducted. You can't decide the rules of a game after the game has been played. How you score has to be clear beforehand. The same is true of evaluation.

The second assumption is that you've allowed time for a pilot program before your program is rolled out extensively. No matter how good you are at sensing needs and developing programs, the second time you do a program is almost twice as good as the first time. Why? Because you learn so much more from doing the real thing. In essence a pilot program is a step in the design process, not the delivery process. It ensnares the use of the best methods of instruction and the best instructor.

A third assumption is evaluation measures results so that we can celebrate our achievements and improve future results.

Now, concerning prerequisites: one prerequisite for effective evaluation is to make sure a complete and thorough needs assessment has been done. Unless we know clearly what the gaps (the difference between where the organization is and where it wants to be) are in the organization and where the gaps are we can't evaluate effectively after training intervention. It is important to have a snapshot of where the participants and the organization were before the intervention took place. The needs assessment is the snapshot.

A second prerequisite is that the people attending and the managers sending people to the training program see a need for the training. It's going to be hard to get anyone to spend time on evaluating something they didn't think was needed in the first place.

A third prerequisite is that people in the organization and the organization itself see training as strategic to the organization. In other words that it plays a significant role in helping the organization get from "where it is now" to "where it wants to be." And that the individual program to be evaluated is seen as a part of that strategy.

A fourth prerequisite is that the training program is linked to the organization's strategic plan. Is the training under consideration seen as something that clearly makes a difference to the organization? If it's not you have some groundwork to lay and you probably want to read books like Dana and Jim Robinson's "Training for Impact - How to Link Training to Business Needs and Measure the Results" or Robert Brinkerhoff's "Achieving Results from Training." In 1994, Resources for Organizations, Inc. will be releasing its book covering a total approach to needs assessment and evaluation as an integrated approach to making an impact with training. A card with your name and address sent to ROI will put you on the advance notice list.

A fifth prerequisite is that the training to be delivered is designed around a set of measurable results and objectives. It is almost impossible to evaluate, in any meaningful way, a program that has no clear outcomes.

A sixth prerequisite is that evaluation is viewed as a process. Improving total results over time and adjusting future programs and follow-up programs must happen in order for the objectives to be met and the results delivered. It is not a statistical exercise in collecting data which is not used.

A seventh prerequisite is that evaluation becomes a marketing tool to generate better support for training. It becomes a marketing tool when there is published feedback on the results that the training is producing. It becomes a marketing tool when it increases the communications and therefore, the awareness of training programs that are making a difference. Finally, it becomes a marketing tool when the results being produced position training as a strategic partner in the organization's growth.

So what is evaluation? Besides being processes that help measure the effectiveness of training, it is a number of other things as well.

It is:

> **exciting.** It helps you see in a concrete way that what you're doing is making a difference.

rewarding. It allows participants and other stakeholders to see that the training they've attended has made a positive difference to themselves and the organization.

on-going. The environment that we work in is ever shifting and changing. Therefore evaluation is an ongoing way to insure that the training we are delivering is in touch with current needs and reality.

a way of assigning accountability for the learning. If we are evaluating not only what people have learned and the skills they can demonstrate, but also the environment within which they apply these things on-the-job and the support systems that enable them to use the training, then we have total accountability for learning and application.

a change tool. We live in an ever changing world. The needs of the organization change. Training is one method of helping people retool to meet changing challenges and opportunities.

part of the organization's Early Warning System. It develops awareness of shifts that can affect the organization. These can then be addressed by new training programs or by other types of strategies including policy changes, placement and recruitment strategies, coaching opportunities and systems changes.

So let's get into the specific "How-to's" of evaluation.

A Foreword by the Author

I wrote this evaluation book because of my own frustrations. After I wrote it other teachers and trainers shared their frustrations with me and I found we had much in common.

The following stories are true examples of a few of the frustrations. It is my hope that this book will reduce some of these frustrations and improve training impact.

JANUARY 1990

The workshop began smoothly. We started on time. All the participants were registered and in their seats. I began the workshop as many trainers do; I outlined my objectives and informed the participants of my workshop expectations. Then I asked: "Do you have any expectations you want covered?" I explained any other expectations would be welcome. People were invited to talk to me right then or during breaks about their "special needs or objectives."

The course topic was time management. An in-house needs assessment revealed many employees recognized a need for time management training. As an independent time management consultant, I was contacted to run an in-house training program. The time management program was two days. The first day ran smoothly. When I left I walked past the bar and waved to six or seven people from my workshop who had stopped for Happy Hour.

The morning of the second day I could sense something was wrong but I couldn't put my finger on the trouble. Twenty minutes before lunch break a young man exploded:

> "When are we going to talk about the problems with this organization," he growled.
>
> "Are you referring to specific time management problems?" I asked.

"No," he flatly stated, "I mean the trouble with the leadership in this organization. We get cost directives all the time - and I'm sick of it. Who do they think we are?"

Another participant raised his hand. "Shut up!" he said to the first individual. "This is a time management workshop and I want to learn. I don't want to spend the afternoon talking about company policies beyond my control. Besides, I've been here 12 years and after a while you start to understand the difficulty of setting company policies."

The company coordinator was not present. The venting began. The same six people I'd seen at happy hour wanted to let everyone know about their anger.

Suddenly it was time for lunch. I sat waiting for lunch with my head in my hands, asking myself what happened.

Later that day the evaluations of the workshop were returned to me. Six people ranked me on the lowest scoring possible with no explanation.

JULY 1991

She was a pro in the communication field. She just finished a workshop for clerical and secretarial positions. It had been 8 months since she started in her job as a training specialist in a medium sized manufacturing company. The company relied heavily on training evaluations to determine effectiveness of seminars and leaders. The department head sat down to review her evaluations.

"It appears you didn't respond to the needs of the secretaries," said the department head. "Out of 30 evaluations, only two people state you met your training objectives. What went wrong?"

"I don't know," she responded. "Up until this point I felt very good about the workshop."

DECEMBER 1992

He glanced through the evaluations from his workshop. His fingers stopped at the evaluation with the low score. Someone in his workshop felt he had performed poorly. The scoring scale was 1-5, with 5 as the highest score. The evaluation he held in his hand had 1's and 2's circled, and no written comments. The trainer thought to himself, "Does this person think I did a bad job or did he/she not read the instructions and assume a "1" score is the highest rating?" He sighed and picked up another evaluation form. This form had a written comment next to the question: How well did the instructor answer your questions? 1-2-3-4-5. The written comment was barely legible: "He didn't answer the question about why documentation is important."

The trainer shook his head and thought: "Why didn't you ask that question? I fielded questions all day. I asked repeatedly for questions from you. I allowed 20 minutes at the end for questions and we only used 10 minutes. Why didn't you ask?"

Chapter I:
Why Evaluate?

THE DEFINITION *Evaluation is the means used to determine the worth or value of the training.*

Organizations need to know whether their investments in training are worth the time, money and effort. Both the organization and the individual decision maker want information about the worth or value of training. Effective evaluation systems can provide information about training effectiveness. Evaluations can answer the following questions:

1. Does the training increase or develop effectiveness in reaching organizational goals or in handling procedures?
2. Does the training improve the worker's performance?
3. Is the training process effective?

The above three questions can be rephrased:

What is the benefit to the organization?

What is the benefit to the worker?

How effective is the training?

These questions are asked by many organizations. The answers to these questions may determine the type, quality and frequency of training. Effective evaluations can answer these questions and provide accountability for trainers and training departments.

In the past, training and evaluation of training have often been viewed as separate processes. For training to be accountable, the training process and the evaluation process need to be an integrated system. Evaluation built into the training process is able to: set ground rules, gather specific data, be effective as a summary, determine learning, determine transference and reveal training effectiveness or areas for improvement.

It is quite easy to amass a range of data through the use of simple measurement techniques. It takes thoughtful planning to gather "critical information;" information which reveals the impact of the training.

If you are considering implementing evaluations, you must ask yourself some questions: "Are we measuring the right stuff?" "What does the information truly reveal?" and "Who interprets the data?"

The first step in determining what to measure is to ask the individuals involved in the training to determine "what they want to know about the training." In other words what knowledge, data or information do they want to receive from the evaluations.

The individuals involved in the training may be: the participants who might want to know "how well the other participants were able to apply the information back on the job," the trainer who might want to know "how much the participants actually learned" or "what the participants suggest to improve the training," the CEO who might want to know if the training is aligned with the companies strategic objectives, the training director who might want to know if the training is cost effective, the supervisor or manager of the participants who might want to know "whether the participant learned something useful which can improve the day-to-day work."

To gather this information, you may want to send survey questions to each of the individuals involved in the "outcomes" of the training and ask them to respond to the question: "What knowledge, data or information do you or your department want to receive about the training which takes place in this organization?" Their answers will direct you to which of the measurement techniques will be most useful for gaining the information your organization can utilize.

Chapter II: Revelations!

WHAT CAN EFFECTIVE EVALUATIONS REVEAL?

Effectively written evaluations can reveal:

1. If learning took place.
2. Participants' entry level.
3. If the training objectives were met.
4. If the facilities met participants' needs.
5. If the facilities met the instructor's needs.
6. If the trainer fulfilled his/her job requirements.
7. How participants plan to use information.
8. Training effectiveness.
9. Areas that need improvement in the training.
10. Future training needs for participants.

WHAT DO PRESENT EVALUATIONS REVEAL?

Many commonly used evaluations merely reveal how pleased the participant is or is not. These evaluations, usually handed out at the end of a workshop, ask the participant for his/her reactions. These "happy quotient" evaluations do not necessarily reveal anything but the participant's emotional state (i.e., happy, sad, glad, angry, frustrated, etc.). The emotional state may or may not have a direct connection with the training experience. This popularity poll type evaluation assumes that popularity and happiness are the outcome of effective training. It is important to take time to ask the question: "Is the participant's immediate happiness reaction an accurate judgment of a training experience?"

Chapter II: Revelations!

Much anecdotal evidence suggests that participants frequently have their highest "happiness reaction" when their view of the world is supported. Yet, the "happiness reaction" appears to lower as the measurement in knowledge gain increases, suggesting that change, learning new ideas or new ways of doing things may have some inherent frustrations which show up in the post-reaction survey.

Several studies, including "The Doctor Fox Lecture: A Paradigm of Education," Vol. 48, July, 1973; and "Broadwell on Instructor Evaluation" by Martin Broadwell from "Training in Business and Industry" October 1991, question the students' abilities to assess the trainers effectiveness during or immediately after a training session.

The post-reaction survey commonly referred to as the "happiness sheet" does have its place in measurement. It is a measure of the satisfaction of the participants. The problem arises when people believe erroneously that the post-reaction survey indicates the learning, the impact or the effectiveness of the training. Trainers must continually remind themselves and others that a post-reaction survey determines ONLY the "satisfaction level of participants."

Chapter II: Revelations!

Many of the commonly used questions in evaluation do not address the training. Some evaluation questions reveal the effectiveness of a needs assessment.

Example: Did the workshop meet your needs?

The answer to this question may reveal more about the needs assessment approach than the effectiveness of a classroom training experience. Technically, this question asks if the workshop objectives met the participant's individual, perhaps personal, needs. In this case the participant's answer may reveal more about the assessment of her/his needs/wants or desires, than about the workshop effectiveness.

Ideally, the organizational goals and objectives are stated and translated into measurable terms. Then a needs assessment is completed to determine which areas warrant training. At this time, personal or individual needs could also be compiled. The training objectives are then developed to respond to the needed areas. The personal or individual needs may be secondary to the organization's perceived need areas. Thus, the participant response to the example questions may reveal effectiveness of the needs assessment approach and whether or not the needs assessment identified the individual need.

What actually happens in the development of needs assessments is often very different. The organizational goals and objectives are rarely translated into measurable terms. The typical needs assessment reveals interest levels or problem areas in work environments. The dart board effect is often used in training departments to meet identified interest levels or problem areas. The dart board effect allows all types of "one shot" training in a hit or miss fashion. The advantage of the dart board effect is that this process appears to respond to the interest levels and problems of the organization.

Dart Board Effect

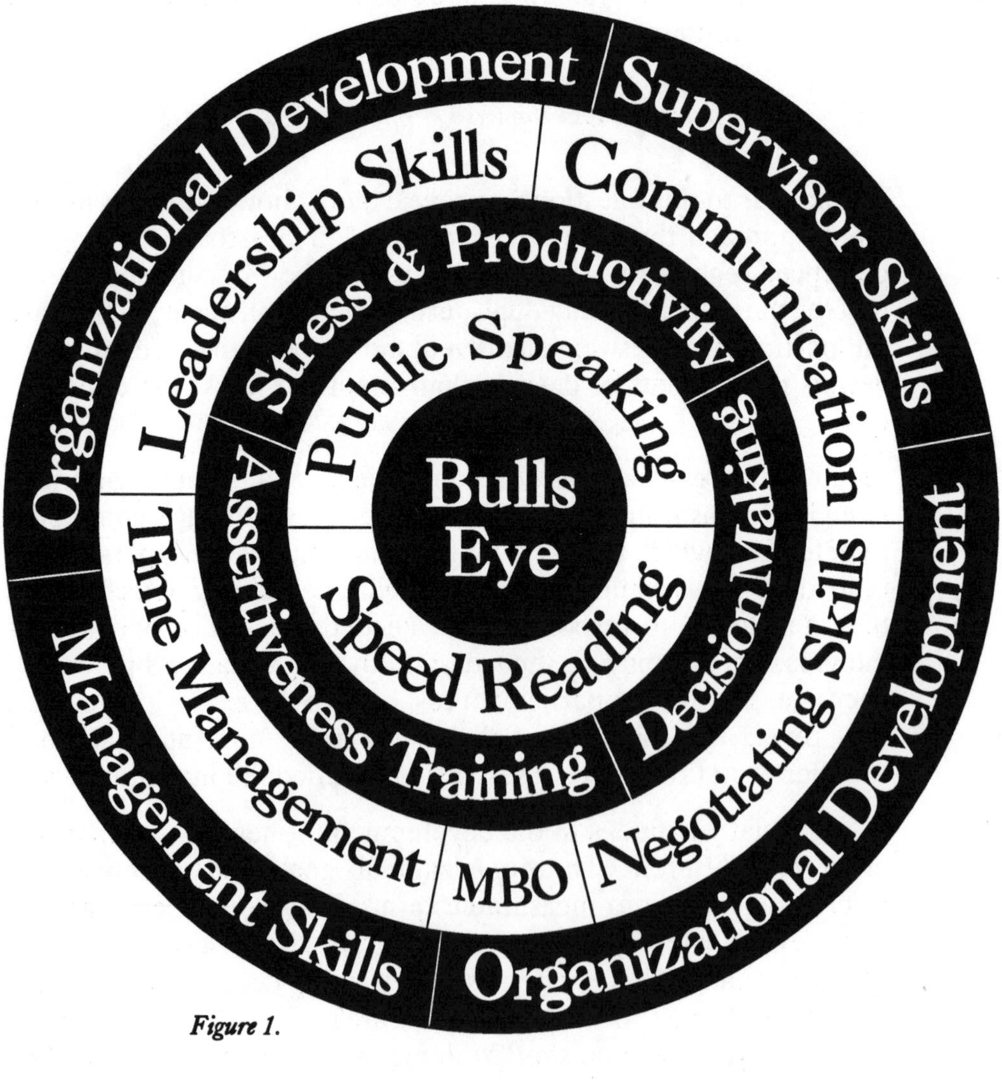

Figure 1.

Actually the process responds to the interests and problems of those people who participated in the needs assessment. The people who participate in the needs assessment may not be the workshop participants. (See figure 1)

Another commonly used process is "Simon Says." The decision maker of the organization believes the workers need training in certain areas and therefore training in those areas is planned. When the "Simon Says" process is used, the participants' answer to the question: "Did the workshop meet your needs?" reveals the accuracy of the decision maker's perceptions.

Evaluations commonly reveal the participant's happiness quotient and the effectiveness of the needs analysis. Needs assessment and translating organizational goals into measurable terms is not the topic of this book.

Because the "ideal" is often out of the trainer's reach, this book is designed to deal with effective evaluation of the classroom training experience. Specifically determining whether the training experience is accomplishing the predetermined objectives.

Chapter III:
Basics of an Evaluation System

There are basically four elements necessary for a classroom training experience:

1. The instructor, trainer, teacher or the person (persons) who is in the leadership role.
2. The topic or content of the program.
3. The participants, audience, workshop members or the people who partake of the learning process.
4. The environment (i.e., chairs, tables, location, noise level, ventilation, audio visuals, etc.)

Effective evaluations consider all four elements when evaluating training, as each element has a direct influence on the training experience.

Most evaluations ask for feedback about 2 or 3 of the elements. Commonly used evaluation forms ask participants to rank or grade the training program and instructor. These types of evaluations are participant biased. The bias occurs in the following assumptions:

1. *Participant entry state.*

   There is a general assumption that participants have an open mind or learning attitude toward the topic and instructor.

2. *Participant background.*

   This is the assumption that participants have the background or experience to evaluate the effectiveness of the workshop.

3. *Participant willingness.*

   This assumes participants have willingly attended the workshop and are responding to specific needs they have personally identified.

4. *Passive learners.*

   This assumes the trainer is in the active role and the participant is in the passive role. In other words, learning is something that is done to the participant by the trainer.

5. *Immediate transference.*

   This assumes the participants are immediately able to assess the practical implications of the training and evaluate its effectiveness before testing it personally.

There are 10 ways or methods which you can use to measure your training impact. Which methods you choose to use in your organization will depend on the answers to the questions you and your organization answered in Chapter I.

The following evaluations system offers you ten techniques for measuring your training impact. In addition, it takes into account the four elements necessary for a classroom training experience.

1. *Pre- and Post-Tests* to evaluate participant learning. This becomes a method to evaluate the participants' knowledge gain.
2. *Participant Self Evaluation* assesses the participants' entry state, willingness to learn and attitudes.
3. *Participant Evaluation* by the instructor is an evaluation the trainer uses to assess the participants' entry state, willingness to learn and attitudes.
4. *Trainer Evaluation* is the evaluation of the trainer/teacher effectiveness as assessed by the participants.
5. *Trainer Self Evaluation* is the trainer's rating of his/her own teaching effectiveness.
6. *Content Evaluation* is the participants' evaluation of the information or seminar topic.

7. *Content Trainer Evaluation* asks the trainer to assess the content of the classroom training.
8. *Facilities Participant Evaluation* is the participants' appraisal of the environment including location, ventilation, temperature, etc.
9. *Facilities Trainer Evaluation* is the trainer's appraisal of the environment.
10. *Work Statement/Follow-up Evaluation* is a method of retrieving information about actual participant transference of workshop information to job performance.

The challenge of evaluation is how to receive valuable feedback in all ten areas without spending enormous amounts of time and money in the evaluation process. The key to effective evaluation lies in training evaluation systems. Integrating evaluation with the training process does not need to take inordinate amounts of time or money. An evaluation system incorporated in the training process does take planning.

Chapter IV: Planning the Evaluation System

Before the workshop begins, the objectives or expectations of each training session are planned. With the workshop objectives planned, the next step usually involves information gathering.

These two steps are involved in any seminar development. Pre- and post-test questions can be easily developed as the content is evolved. Integrating an evaluation system begins as soon as the objectives are stated and the content of the workshop set forth.

To assess participant learning in connection with course content, a pre- and post-test is valuable. To construct pre- and post-tests, review the course content and assemble forty to fifty questions about the content. It is important to develop two questions about every topic area, so that one question can appear on the pre-test and the other question on the post-test. To randomly select which of the two questions will appear on the pre-test, flip a coin. There is a disagreement among trainers as to the best type of pre/post- test questions. Multiple choice, fill in the blank and true/false are commonly preferred. Because of the time factor, many trainers prefer true/false. A combination of question types with heavy emphasis on true/false questions appears to be most effective pre/post-test. See figure 2 for a suggested question format.

After 50 questions are developed choose half the questions from each question category by random sampling. In other words, choose at random from 50 questions - 17 true/false questions, 4 multiple choice questions and 4 fill in the blank questions. The first 25 randomly chosen questions will be the pre-test. The second 25 will be the post-test.

In the 40 question sample pre/post-test format, twenty questions will be randomly selected for the pre-test; 15 true/false questions, 5 multiple choice or matching. The remaining 20 questions are the post-test.

Suggested Pre/Post Test Development Format:

50 Question Sample:	
34 Questions	True False
8 Questions	Multiple Choice
8 Questions	Fill In the Blank or Match the Correct Answer

40 Question Sample:	
30 Questions	True False
5 Questions	Multiple Choice
5 Questions	Fill In the Blank or Match the Correct Answer

Figure 2.

The same set of pre/post-test questions are commonly used in training sessions to assess learning. As the participants may recall the pre-test, the post-test often assesses the participants' memory skills, not the knowledge gained. Because of this tendency, a 40-50 question format with randomly selected pre/post-test questions is an effective method of evaluating learning.

The pre-test need take no more than 5-10 minutes. The total time for pre- and post-testing need be no more than 15-19 minutes.

The disadvantage of the typical pre/post-test method is the pre-test often sensitizes the participants to the post-test questions, when the same pre-test questions are used for the post-test. The problem of sensitizing the participants can be partially resolved by using different pre- and post-test questions selected at random as described earlier in this chapter. The participants may be sensitized to the subject matter by the pre-test, but not to the post-test questions. This appears to be the most feasible design to assess knowledge gain, although there are other options. The other options are more costly and usually not adaptable to the one workshop experience. However, in situations with more flexibility the Randomized Control Design might be used. In this design, a control group would be given the pre- and post-tests without the benefit of training. It is important to obtain a control group with the same characteristics as the training group. One method of achieving this would be as follows; assume 70 people register for a seminar but the seminar limit is 30 people. Randomly choose 30 people to attend the workshop, and 30 people to be the control group. The control group will take the pre- and post-tests without the benefit of the workshop. The 30 participants will take the pre-test and post-test with the benefit of the seminar experience. By comparing the control group's tests with the participants' tests, it is now possible to identify changes in the participants that can be attributed reasonably to the seminar.

Tabulating Pre/Post Tests:

Equations are used to tabulate the index of learning for pre- and post-test scores. The result of using these equations will be a measurement of participant learning. The key below explains the symbols used in each equation.

THE KEY: Symbols and Definitions

Symbol		*Definition*
i	=	the participant
x_i	=	the participant's pre-test score
y_i	=	the participant's post-test score
d_i	=	the difference $y_i - x_i$ for the i-th person
$\bar{d}$	=	the average of the d_i computed
n	=	total number of participants
S	=	a standard statistical scale factor *(standard error of the mean)*
t	=	index of learning

Figure 3.

The following equations are used to tabulate pre/post-test scores:

1. $$\bar{d} = \frac{d_1 + d_2 + d_3 \ldots + d_n}{n}$$

2. $$\sqrt{\frac{\sum_{i=1}^{n} (d_i - \bar{d})^2}{n\,(n-1)}} = S$$

3. $$\bar{d} / S = t$$

Example of Tabulation:

Column No.	1	2	3	4
	Pre-test	Post-test	Difference d_i	d_i^2
Person 1	10	15	5	25
Person 2	15	14	-1	1
Person 3	5	20	15	225
Person 4	3	10	7	49
		Totals	26	300

Figure 4.

Suppose for simplicity that four people attend the workshop and obtain pre/post-test scores as given in the first two columns of Figure 4. First, construct the third column of Figure 4 by subtracting each person's pre-test score from his/her post-test score. (These numbers are the d_i's). Next square each difference to produce a column analogous to the fourth column in table 1. Finally, total columns 3 and 4.

This provides the basic information for computing the index of learning, t.

The $\bar{d}$, or average of the d_i's computed, is simply the total of column 3 divided by the total number of participants.

In this case:

$$\bar{d} = \frac{d_1 + d_2 + d_3 + d_4}{n} \qquad \bar{d} = \frac{5 + (-1) + 15 + 7}{4} \qquad \bar{d} = \frac{26}{4} \qquad \bar{d} = 6.5$$

The steps in calculating **S** are:

$$\mathbf{S} = \sqrt{\frac{\sum_{i=1}^{n} (d_i - \bar{d})^2}{n\,(n-1)}} = \sqrt{\frac{d_1^2 + d_2^2 + \ldots + d_n^2 - (d_1 + d_2 + \ldots + d_n)^2/n}{n\,(n-1)}}$$

$$= \sqrt{\frac{300 - (26)^2/4}{4(3)}} = \sqrt{\frac{300 - 169}{12}} = \sqrt{10.92} = 3.3$$

$\mathbf{t} = \bar{d}/S = 6.5/3.3 = 1.97$ The index of learning is then $\mathbf{t = 1.97}$.

Tabulation Results

0 1.5 2 2.5 3

S is always larger than or equal to zero. It will be zero only if all differences are identical. A negative value for S^2 indicates acomputational error.*

0 - 1.5	Chance, little or no evidence of learning
1.5 - 2	Some evidence of learning
2 - 3	Strong evidence of learning
over 3	Very strong evidence of learning

* If you obtain a negative value, rework the computations.

figure 5.

Chapter V: Evaluation Systems: Planning the Ground Rules

Previously the responsibilities for successful classroom training have fallen totally on the shoulders of the trainer. The trainer definitely has responsibilities in the training experience, but so does the participant. Many trainers relate frustrating experiences with the folded-arm participant whose attitude can be summed up: "Just see if you can teach me anything. I dare you!" Yet, trainers have been held responsible for the overall participant response in evaluations, as if the trainer had total control in molding the adult participant. Anyone with training experience knows that the audience can make or break a training experience.

Actors and actresses have known about this phenomenon from stage experiences. They label audiences "hot and cold." A "hot audience" laughs, cries, applauds and generally gives the actors feedback. This feedback fuels the actor's performance and an actor is able to "become greater than himself" or perform seemingly above his abilities. The "cold audience" does not give feedback. They are, for the most part, polite and silent. This zero feedback also influences the actor's performance. The actor has to work harder. The lines may not come as easily. The timing is slower and in general the actor finds it more difficult to perform.

This phenomenon influences trainers also. When the participants accept some responsibility for the success of a training experience the training process becomes more effective.

The question is, "how to get participants to accept some responsibility for the training experience?" To answer this question it is necessary to identify rights and responsibilities of participants and trainers.

In the space provided below take a moment and identify the rights and responsibilities of participants and trainers.

I. Identify and list the responsibilities of a classroom trainer. (Recognizing there are many topic areas involved in this task, please discuss "general responsibilities.")

II. Identify and list the responsibilities of a participant in a classroom training experience.

The effective evaluation system asks the participant to acknowledge his/her responsibilities. Built into the initial training introduction is the Training Rights and Responsibilities. The trainer explains his/her rights and responsibilities and also addresses the expected rights and responsibilities for participants. The use of Training Rights and Responsibilities has three advantages.

1. To set up mutual behavioral expectations for trainer and participants.
2. To serve as a contract between participants and trainer.
3. To define seminar guidelines upon which evaluations can be based.

For participants to evaluate training, there must be some guidelines. The Training Rights and Responsibilities become a method of defining guidelines or responsibilities. Trainers frequently discuss expectations with participants but the responsibilities of the participants are often nebulous.

The Rights and Responsibilities Worksheet on the following page offers some suggestions for developing seminar rights and responsibilities. Using your responsibility lists from page 26 and this guideline, develop your own Rights and Responsibilities checklist on page 27.

Rights and Responsibilities Worksheet:

Seminar Guidelines

Instructor:

1. The Trainer's Responsibilities

   a. Speak clearly

   b. Keep training session moving and on course

   c. Answer questions, clarify, explain

   d. Actively involve the participants

   e. Know training materials thoroughly

   f. Announce breaks and stay on schedule

2. Responsibilities for Content

   a. Clearly organized

   b. Use examples and clarify

   c. Provide necessary data

   d. Use examples as relevant as possible

   e. State course objectives

   f. Well prepared

   g. Adaptable

Participants:

1. The Participant's Responsibilities

   a. Listen, be attentive

   b. Not side track seminar with inappropriate behavior

   c. Ask or be willing to give feedback, to say, "I need more information," "I don't understand," etc.

   d. Be willing to participate in exercises or discussions

   e. Have the right to disagree and verbalize that disagreement, but not to stop workshop

   f. Return from breaks on time

2. Responsibilities for Content

   a. Keep an open mind until complete ideas are presented

   b. Adapt or transfer information into meaningful examples. (The instructor will use as many relevant examples as possible, but can't possibly give examples for every situation or position

   c. Course objectives are stated in general-participants are responsible to seek out instructor to modify course objectives if they do not meet participant's needs

Rights and Responsibilities Worksheet:

Seminar Guidelines

Instructor:

1. The Trainer's Responsibilities

   a. ____________________

   b. ____________________

   c. ____________________

   d. ____________________

   e. ____________________

   f. ____________________

2. Responsibilities for Content

   a. ____________________

   b. ____________________

   c. ____________________

   d. ____________________

   e. ____________________

   f. ____________________

Participants:

1. The Participant's Responsibilities

   a. ____________________

   b. ____________________

   c. ____________________

   d. ____________________

   e. ____________________

   f. ____________________

2. Responsibilities for Content

   a. ____________________

   b. ____________________

   c. ____________________

   d. ____________________

   e. ____________________

   f. ____________________

Integrating the Rights and Responsibilities into the training is important. Please take a moment and develop your plan for integrating the Rights and Responsibilities in your training. Be sure to address when you will do it? How you plan to do it? What conflicts you foresee? etc.

Chapter VI: Post Workshop Participant Evaluations

After a training session, many participants are thinking about their personal time commitments. Some begin thinking about home responsibilities. Some participants may think about a relaxing evening. Whatever they are thinking about, they are preparing their thoughts to leave the workshop.

Because most participants are concerned about leaving the workshop "on time," it is important to have a visually well-prepared post-workshop evaluation. An evaluation needs to "look" like it is brief, preferably one page, to get full participant response.

From the trainer's point of view the evaluation needs to be effective at gathering data. Therefore a successful post-work evaluation form needs to satisfy the participant and the trainer by:

1. Being brief and able to be done quickly.
2. Gathering many types of information.

The evaluation sample is an example of a brief evaluation that gathers different types of meaningful information. (See figure 6)

The first five questions ask participants about their rights and responsibilities. These five questions ask the participants to respond to the overall question:

Did you do your part in this learning experience?

An additional question (not shown in Figure 6) can be asked to gather further information about participant entry state. This question can be phrased:

Were there any outside influences that affected your ability to appreciate this workshop?

Common answers to this question are: “I didn’t feel well.” “I’m getting a divorce and I couldn’t think today.” “I had an argument with my child this morning and I can’t get it out of my head.”

These first questions may serve as a screening device for participant entry state. As such the evaluations with “no” answers to these questions may be pulled from the general evaluation tabulation and tabulated separately.

Questions 6-10 ask for feedback about the seminar leader. These five questions ask the participant to respond to the overall question:

Was the trainer effective?

In questions 11-14, the objectives for the workshop need to be stated in the evaluation. These questions ask the participants whether or not the workshop objectives were met.

Questions 11-15 ask the participants to assess the course content.

Question 16 asks about the training environment.

Question 17 asks the participants to rate the workshop on a scale of poor to excellent. This question serves to test the other questions. For example, a participant could respond that he/she did not believe the objectives were covered, but circle an “excellent”; indicating the workshop was very useful. The participant in effect would be saying: “Although the objectives were not covered the workshop was very useful.”

This simple one page evaluation evaluates all four workshop elements: the participants, the trainer, the content and the environment as perceived by the participant.

Sample Evaluation Form

Check One: Yes / No

(1) Was it your choice to attend this workshop? ____ ____

(2) Did you listen attentively to the information presented? ____ ____
If you responded NO to question 2, explain________________________

(3) Did you arrive on time and return from breaks punctually? ____ ____
If you responded NO, explain________________________

(4) Did you participate willingly in the workshop activities? ____ ____
If you responded NO, explain________________________

(5) Did you have an acceptable attitude that facilitated learning? ____ ____
If NO, explain________________________

(6) Did the seminar leader allow time for questions? ____ ____
If you answered NO; did you ask the leader questions? ____ ____

(7) Did the seminar leader explain and clarify his/her information? ____ ____
If NO, did you ask the leader to clarify or explain further? ____ ____

(8) Did the seminar leader speak clearly and distinctly? ____ ____
If NO, explain________________________

(9) Did the seminar leader keep the training session moving and on course? ____ ____
If NO, explain________________________

(10) Did the instructor demonstrate a thorough knowledge of the topic? ____ ____
If NO, give examples.________________________

(11) Was the following objective covered in this seminar: ____ ____
(Objective #1)________________________
If NO, explain________________________

(12) Was the following objective covered in this seminar: ____ ____
(Objective #2)________________________
If NO, explain________________________

(13) Was the following objective covered in this seminar: ____ ____
(Objective #3)________________________
If NO, explain________________________

(14) Was the following objective covered in this seminar: ____ ____
(Objective #4)________________________
If NO, explain________________________

(15) Was the course content clearly organized and well prepared? ____ ____
If NO, explain________________________

(16) Were the facilities adequate? ____ ____
If NO, explain________________________

(17) Rate this workshop: Please circle one:
Poor Fair Good Very Good Excellent

(18) Please add general comments:________________________

figure 6.

The participant evaluation form is only a sample of how an evaluation form can be written. What questions would you or your organization like to ask the participants that the evaluation sample does not ask?

Chapter VII:
Post Workshop Leader Evaluations

The "Evaluation by Seminar Leader" asks the trainer to assess the four workshop elements: the participants, the trainer, the content and the environment. (See Figure 7.) Questions 1-5 ask the seminar leader to evaluate the participants in relation to their rights and responsibilities. Questions 6-10 ask the seminar leader to assess his/her own performance. Questions 11-13 ask the trainer to evaluate the course content and whether the objectives were all met. Question 14 asks about the environment; room set up, ventilation, room size, food, etc.

Evaluations by Trainers are not usually used with the frequency of the Evaluations by Participants. A complete evaluation system includes the trainer's assessments in the evaluation input.

The "Evaluation by Seminar Leader" is only a sample of how an evaluation form can be written. What questions do you or your organization want the trainer to answer that the evaluation sample doesn't ask?

Sample Evaluation by Trainer

		Yes	No
(1)	Did the participants listen attentively? If NO, explain______	____	____
(2)	Did participants arrive and return from breaks on time? If NO, detail______	____	____
(3)	Did participants participate willingly in seminar activities? If NO, give examples______	____	____
(4)	Did participants have an acceptable attitude to facilitate learning? If NO, explain______	____	____
(5)	Were participants willing to ask questions and give feedback? If NO, give details______ ______	____	____
(6)	Did you allow time for questions and feedback? If NO, explain______	____	____
(7)	Do you feel you explained and clarified your information thoroughly? If NO explain______ ______	____	____
(8)	Do you feel you kept the seminar moving and on course? If NO, explain______	____	____
(9)	Do you feel you demonstrated a thorough knowledge of the topic? If NO, explain______	____	____
(10)	Do you feel you spoke clearly and distinctly? If NO, explain ______	____	____
(11)	Did you state the workshop objectives? If NO, explain______	____	____
(12)	Do you believe you fulfilled each objective? If NO, state the objective(s) not fulfilled and explain why______ ______ ______ ______	____	____
(13)	Do you feel the course content was organized and well-prepared? If NO, explain______ ______ ______ ______	____	____
(14)	Were the facilities adequate? If NO, explain______ ______	____	____
(15)	General Comments ______ ______ ______		

figure 7.

Chapter VIII: The Follow-Up

What actually happens when a participant leaves the workshop? Does he or she attempt to implement the new information gleaned from the workshop experience, or is the information remembered, perhaps understood, but not implemented?

A seasoned trainer tells the following story:

At the beginning of a time management workshop a participant approached the trainer and stated: "I've already been to three time management workshops!" The trainer wondered "why" the participant came to his Time Management Workshop after having attended three previously. Certainly after three workshops the participant must understand the basics of time management. The trainer asked: "Do you have anything in mind you specifically want to get out of today's session?" The participant answered, "Oh, I understand all about making lists and setting priorities. What I want to find out is how you do it, how you stick to your number one priority, and how you implement this stuff?"

Are the participants able to implement their new knowledge? To effectively evaluate this, a follow-up system is easily put to use. The follow-up system asks several questions:

1. What information was valuable?
2. What do you plan to do with this information?
    a. In what situation will you attempt to implement your knowledge?
    b. What is your "implementing plan"?

The most productive time in a workshop to introduce the work-statement follow-up is during the summary. Hopefully, the work-statement will have a brief topical outline of the information presented in the workshop. The summary stimulates the participants to consider the entire content in developing their implementation plans. Without the outline participants frequently concentrate on implementing the "last" thought provoking ideas covered in the seminar. By asking participants to address When? Where? and How? they plan to apply their knowledge or skill, the work-statement focuses participants' attention on the use or implementation of workshop materials.

See figure 8 for a sample of a work-statement follow-up form. A 9 1/2 by 4 1/2 inch envelope needs to be included with the follow-up form. When participants complete the form they are asked to address the envelope to themselves and place the work-statement in the addressed envelope. At this time it is important to inform the participants that their work-statements will be sent to them in approximately three to four weeks.

The work-statement follow-up accomplishes two tasks. First, the participants may work harder to implement their plans as they know they will be asked "how they did" in three to four weeks. Second, the work-statement will supply valuable data on participants' abilities to apply workshop materials.

In three to four weeks the work-statement form (Figure 8) is sent to the participant with the follow-up instructions (Figure 10) and a smaller return envelope. If a return envelope is supplied, there is a greater probability participants will return the forms.

There are optional phases of follow-up evaluations. A long term follow-up may be utilized in six to seven months. Copies of the work-statement and follow-up instructions would be sent again. Then the six-month response can be compared with the three-week response.

Another optional follow-up adaptation is the supervisor follow-up. With participants permission, a copy of the work-statement can be sent immediately following the workshop to the supervisor. In approximately three to four weeks, the work-statement (Figure 8) plus the Supervisor Follow-up instructions (Figure 11) are sent to the supervisor for evaluation. The advantage of this option is in retaining the supervisor's support during the initial implementation process. The disadvantage is the supervisor may become critical during the implementation process. The question of whether or not to use this option lies with the participant. The participant must be comfortable with supervisor involvement.

A less threatening option to involve the supervisor is the Supervisor Alert Card. The postcard merely gives background and asks for support. (See Figure 9.)

Sample Work Statement Form

Describe situations where you plan to apply this material and tell when and how you plan to apply it. Be specific.

COURSE OUTLINE	IMPLEMENTATION GOALS	Do Not Write In This Column
I. ______________ ______________ ______________	Situation:______________ ______________ My plan to apply:__________ ______________ ______________	A______ B______ C______
II. ______________ ______________ ______________	Situation:______________ ______________ My plan to apply: __________ ______________ ______________	A______ B______ C______
III. ______________ ______________ ______________	Situation:______________ ______________ My plan to apply:__________ ______________ ______________	A______ B______ C______
IV. ______________ ______________ ______________	Situation:______________ ______________ My plan to apply:__________ ______________ ______________	A______ B______ C______
V. ______________ ______________ ______________	Situation:______________ ______________ My plan to apply:__________ ______________ ______________	A______ B______ C______

Please address the attached envelope to yourself as it will be returned to you in approximately 3 weeks.

figure 8.

SUPERVISOR ALERT CARD

Dear Supervisor,

________________________ has taken a workshop dealing with________________________________ ___________________. During the next few weeks he/she will be attempting to adapt these ideas and skills to be more successful on the job. Please offer your support during this time.

Sincerely,

figure 9.

Sample Form for Follow-Up Instructions

Please review the course content. Then review what you had planned to apply.

Were you able to apply your plans? For each situation there is adjacent A____________________ B____________________ and C____________________ located under the column headed "Do not write in this column." You may now write in the A, B, or C column. If you were able to apply your plan successfully, check A on your work-statement evaluation.

If you were partially able to apply your plan and are still working on the implementation, check B. If you were not able to successfully apply your plan, check C, and please explain what obstacles stopped your application.

Obstacles that stopped successful application:

____

____

____

____

____

____

Please feel free to make any additional comments about the workshop or yourself on this paper.

____

____

____

____

____

____

figure 10.

Sample Form for Follow-Up Instructions

________________________ was a participant in a workshop dealing with ________________________. During the last three to four weeks he/she has attempted to implement the ideas or skills listed on the enclosed sheet labeled Work-Statement Follow-Up. Please review what he/she has written. Did you observe any change? For each situation there is an adjacent A________________________ B________________________ and C________________________, located under the column headed "Do not write in this column." Please use this column now. If you were able to note a change, any change, please check A. If you were able to note some effort to change, check B. If you were not able to note a change or an effort to change, check C.

Were you able to offer your support to this person as they attempted to implement their actions?

Yes__________ No__________

Please feel free to add any additional comments.______________

____

____

____

____

____

____

____

____

____

figure 11.

Chapter IX:
Implementing the Evaluation System

The evaluation system and the seminar work as a unit. In many workshops the attitude is: "The seminar is over, now let's evaluate." The evaluations must become part of the training to be truly effective and efficient. The evaluation facilitates transference and asks for examination of what has taken place. A great philosopher once said "The unexamined life is not worth living." Perhaps that is true of training experiences. The evaluation or examination determines the worth.

To mold the evaluation system with the training process it is important to understand the time sequence. Figure 12 is a sample of how a standard one day workshop could implement the evaluation system. Note that the evaluation system becomes an integrated part of the workshop.

Evaluation System Sample

Event	Time/Explanation
Workshop begins	8:30
Introduction and Pre-test	If the pre-test is already handed out it should take 5-7 minutes.
Objectives are stated	Part of workshop content
Explain Rights and Responsibilities	3-6 minutes
Workshop continues as planned	4-6 hours
Workshop summary with Job/Work statements	Part of workshop allow 15-20 minutes for Job/Work statements
Post test	5-10 minutes
Seminar Evaluation by participants	5-7 minutes
Workshop ends	
Seminar Evaluation by leader	5-7 minutes
Follow-up	3-4 weeks later

figure 12.

Chapter IX: Implementing the Evaluation System

Now that you have considered the components of an effective evaluation system you need to determine what will be the best evaluation techniques for you and your organization. Do you want an evaluation system? To decide if an evaluation system meets your needs, please answer the following questions:

1. How much time will you spare in a day's training for evaluations to be completed?____________________

2. How will the evaluations affect future training?____________________

3. Who will see the evaluations?____________________

4. What is the purpose of your evaluations?____________________

5. What type of commitment will you make to develop your evaluations?____________________

6. What is the first step you will take in implementing an evaluation system?____________________

7. What advantages can you anticipate in using an evaluation system?____________________

8. Can you anticipate any disadvantages in using an evaluation system?____________________

Summary of Workshop Tabulations

The chart shown in Figure 13 summaries the results of the participants' evaluation, the pre and post testing date and the work-statement follow-ups. This summary, when considered with the leaders evaluation, provides a reasonable measure of training effectiveness.

Workshop Seminar Title: ____________________

Date of Workshop: ____________ Seminar Leader: ____________

Number of Participants: ____________ Location: ____________

	Percent of Screening Questions with Indicated Percent of "NO" Response		
	0	*1 - 2*	*3 or more*
Percent of "YES" on questions #6 and #15			
Average response to question #17			
Index of learning			
Average difference $\bar{d}$			
Percent of A's on work statement			
Percent of B's on work statement			
Percent of C's on work statement			
Number of "YES" responses to question #16			

figure 13.

Chapter X:
Evaluation Questions and Why They Don't Work

Sample One

Please circle the response closest to your opinion about this course.	Very strongly DISAGREE	Strongly DISAGREE	Generally DISAGREE	Generally AGREE	Strongly AGREE	Very strongly AGREE	Most strongly AGREE
The instructor made the course interesting.	1	2	3	4	5	6	7
The course content met my high expectations.	1	2	3	4	5	6	7
Rate the teaching technique used.	1	2	3	4	5	6	7

figure 14.

The seven scale rating system is a common form used for workshop or seminar evaluation. There are several basic disadvantages with this form of evaluation:

1. The 1-7 rating scale asks for fine distinctions which may not be clear in the participant's mind. What is the difference between very strongly agree and most strongly agree? If I agree, how do I rate my agreement on a four-part scale? The 1-7 scale may be meaningful to the people who developed the scale but the numbers lose much of their significance if they are not meaningful to the participants. Be careful of asking for too fine distinctions of your participants.

2. The wording of the questions is important. The way a question is worded may affect the participant's response. For example, the second question in Sample One (Figure 14) refers to "high expectations." How should participants respond if they came to

the workshop with low expectations? The use of the word high to modify expectations makes this a leading question, similar to, "When did you stop beating your spouse?" The third question is also worded to affect the participants' response. What are teaching techniques? Because a person is a participant in a workshop we should not assume he/she has a basic knowledge of teaching techniques? The words "teaching techniques" need to be defined or explained to guarantee participants' understanding.

3. Check the assumptions that underlie your questions. Ask yourself, "Is this really what I want to ask?" The first question in Sample One has an underlying assumption that can be stated this way: It is the instructor's responsibility to make the course interesting, as participants are not responsible for interest in the materials. The second question makes the assumption that participants arrived with high expectations. As people are different so are people's expectations and it is unreasonable to generalize expectations of participants. The third question assumes participants have a background in education or training. To rate teaching techniques, a participant must first recognize what those techniques are: lecture, triads, role playing, case studies, games, discussion, etc. Then the participant needs to compare how these techniques were used. To compare techniques, one needs at least something to "compare with." Thus a further assumption is made that the participants have attended similar workshops and have observed similar teaching techniques.

Sample Two

Did this workshop meet my needs and objectives?	1	2	3	4	5
Was the instructor knowledgeable about the topic?	1	2	3	4	5
Will I be able to apply the content directly to my job?	1	2	3	4	5
Would you recommend this course to a friend, co-worker or supervisor?	1	2	3	4	5
Were the meeting facilities satisfactory?	1	2	3	4	5

figure 15.

Sample Two (Figure 15) is the most commonly used type of evaluation form for seminars. It asks participants to distinguish ratings on a scale from 1-5. The five sample questions include the five that are:

1. Were you happy and satisfied?
2. Did the instructor do a good job?
3. Will the information be useful on your job?
4. Would you recommend the course?
5. Was the food, meeting room, etc., satisfactory?

There are, of course, various ways to ask these five questions and there are frequently other types of questions included in an evaluation form, but these appear to be the most common. There are several disadvantages with this type of form.

First, there is a strong tendency for people to have a "response pattern." They tend to choose answers from the same "area" or range of numbers. This may vary from choosing answers from the middle of the numbers (see Figure 16) to choosing answers from either end of the numbers (See Figure 17)

Mid-reponse Pattern

Did this workshop meet my needs and objectives?	1	2	(3)	4	5
Was the instructor knowledgeable about the topic?	1	2	3	(4)	5
Will I be able to apply the content directly to my job?	1	2	(3)	4	5
Would you recommend this course to a friend, co-worker or supervisor?	1	2	(3)	4	5
Were the meeting facilities satisfactory?	1	(2)	3	4	5

↑ *figure 16.*

High-reponse Pattern

Did this workshop meet my needs and objectives?	1	2	3	(4)	5
Was the instructor knowledgeable about the topic?	1	2	3	4	(5)
Will I be able to apply the content directly to my job?	1	2	3	(4)	5
Would you recommend this course to a friend, co-worker or supervisor?	1	2	3	4	(5)
Were the meeting facilities satisfactory?	1	2	3	(4)	5

Low-reponse Pattern

Did this workshop meet my needs and objectives?	(1)	2	3	4	5
Was the instructor knowledgeable about the topic?	1	(2)	3	4	5
Will I be able to apply the content directly to my job?	(1)	2	3	4	5
Would you recommend this course to a friend, co-worker or supervisor?	(1)	2	3	4	5
Were the meeting facilities satisfactory?	1	(2)	3	4	5

figure 17.

Second, there is no way to tell whether the answers have been well thought out. How can you determine from numbers, briefly circled, whether the answer was thoughtful or received no thought at all. Several seminar leaders have had experiences of receiving all low marks on an evaluation form, then receiving a quick comment at the bottom of the evaluation stating: Excellent workshop!! Did the participant fail to read the instructions or not give thought to the questions?

Third, the questions themselves affect the response. The first question, "Did this workshop meet my needs and objectives?" has little to do with the evaluation of the seminar. Essentially it is a two part question: 1) asking self-evaluation of needs and objectives or "What were your needs and objectives?" 2) asking the participant to discriminate as to how closely personal needs matched the workshop content or "Did the workshop content match your personal objectives or needs?" If this question has any validity it is only as a method of evaluating the needs assessment, not the workshop.

Example: Because of a hiring freeze, Supervisor A is working overtime 3-4 times a week to complete job tasks. The company training department, through the use of a company-wide needs assessment tool, has determined a need for time management training. The training department contacts XYZ Consultants and hires them to teach time management. The training department sends out notices to all supervisors informing them of the scheduled time management workshop. Supervisor A sees the notice and attends. Supervisor A discovers she manages her time quite well according to the seminar. She is frustrated because she still has to work 3-4 nights a week to keep up with the job. Supervisor A's need was to find a way not to work overtime. The objectives of the time management course were to teach effective time usage skills. As long as the company continues the hiring freeze, Supervisor A will need to work overtime. When Supervisor A responds to her evaluation, she ranks question one "Did this workshop meet your needs and objectives?" as low as possible, even though the workshop met the time management objectives. The response reveals Supervisor A's anger at her company's policies instead of her appraisal of the workshop.

It is common for participants to arrive at a workshop with hidden agendas. Is it the trainer's responsibility to reveal hidden agendas, meet personal needs and accomplish seminar objectives? Does a participant have any responsibility in this process? Evaluation question number one is written so that responsibilities for "meeting needs" become the trainer's. This slant may affect the participant's answer.

There is no clear basis for responding to the question: "Was the instructor knowledgeable about the topic?" How does a participant assess an instructor's knowledge? By credentials, ability to speak understandably about the topic, ability to answer questions about the topic, ability to respond to written testing about the topic or background in the topic field? Hopefully an instructor's knowledge will be assessed by those in charge before the workshop. During a workshop, participants may be able to assess the instructor's skill in presenting information, but this has little to do with the sum total of an instructor's knowledge.

Question three asks for a quick response to a complex question. When learning new information people need time to internalize or think through their new ideas. The ideas may have to simmer for a period of time before they are useable to the individual. This question assumes participants are making immediate transference of new information to an old situation, the job. In question number three the word "directly" implies that the content of the course has immediate coherence or cohesion to the job position. The assumption of "immediate cohesion" contradicts basic theories about the change process. It is generally accepted that most changes in human lives which come about through learning are gradual, not immediate.

Thus, question three asks for a type of fore-knowledge or future seeing. "Will you be able to apply this?" asks for information about the future as to 1) the participant's abilities, 2) the work environment, 3) the supervisor's attitude, as all three affect the participant's application on the job.

Example: Participant B takes assertiveness training. At the end of the workshop he is asked, "Will you be able to directly apply assertiveness training to your job?" Participant B is very thoughtful and circles number 1 or the low degree of response. Does this mean the workshop failed? Not necessarily. When participant B thought about the question, he considered himself. He knows himself. He has been shy and untalkative all his life. Just thinking about being assertive with his aggressive shop foreman makes his stomach turn. Therefore, participant B circles the lowest response. If questioned weeks later, it is possible that he may have used some of his assertiveness training on the job, but it was after he digested the information and allowed time for change.

Therefore, question three actually scores the transference ability of the participants, but says little about the program content.

Question four mixes response data. Perhaps I would recommend the program to a co-worker, but I do not believe it is applicable for my supervisor. Which number should I circle? In fact a 1-5 scale is inappropriate for this question. "Would you recommend this course" asks for a yes or no answer. Either you would recommend it or you wouldn't.

Question five, "Were the meeting facilities adequate?" requires a yes or no response. The question asks were the facilities satisfactory scored on a 1-5 scale. Does circling a number one mean they were satisfactory to a low degree?

It is impossible to give an example of every evaluation question in use. Hopefully these samples have pointed out some standard pitfalls. The checklist below (Figure 18) may be helpful in avoiding some of those pitfalls.

Checklist for Questions in an Evaluation

- ☐ 1. Does this question ask for fine distinctions in scoring?
- ☐ 2. Are there any words that load or color the question?
- ☐ 3. Does this question ask for too quick a response to a complex area?
- ☐ 4. Does this question ask for future seeing?
- ☐ 5. Are the question's assumptions valid?
- ☐ 6. Do the participants have the background to answer this question?
- ☐ 7. Are all the terms used in the question clear?
- ☐ 8. Is this question directly related to the seminar evaluation?
- ☐ 9. Is there a clear basis for responding to this question?

figure 18.

Chapter XI: Developing Evaluation Questions

Skillful questions can reveal the effectiveness of classroom training, but asking skillful questions is an art. To ask skillful questions, it is important to understand question types.

The probing or open-ended question asks the participant to express what is on his/her mind. This question cannot be answered with a yes or no. Frequently these questions start with: What, how, who, when or where. The following questions are examples:

1. What comments would you like to make about this seminar?
2. What have you learned or gained from this experience?
3. What information was most useful?
4. How do you plan to implement your projects?

There are basically three advantages to the open-ended questions. First, from the evaluator's perception, these question types are relatively easy to write. Second, these questions allow for a large range of answers from the participant. Third, the question probes the participant to find out what he/she is thinking.

The disadvantages are five-fold. First, it takes a longer amount of time for the participants to answer the open-ended question. Second, the participants may not give complete information in their answers. Without complete information an answer may be misleading. Third, participants may not answer at all because of the amount of writing involved. Fourth, there may be no means to analyze the data because of the variety of answers. Instead of useable data, the answer results in a listing of comments. The fifth disadvantage relates to participant internal and external environments. The open-ended question asks the participants to express their thinking. Those thoughts may be directly connected to the participant's: a.) physical comfort at the time of testing, b.) attitude about the seminar leader, c.) relationship to co-workers present, or even relationships at home. The open-ended question, by asking the participants to express their feelings, ideas, thinking, etc., invites the participants to more subjectivity.

The two choice questions direct a participant to a specific subject area. Frequently these questions can be answered "no" or "yes," (or "true" or "false.") The following question is an example:

> Did the seminar leader keep the workshop moving and on course? Yes_________ No_________

The advantages of the two choice question are three-fold. First, the participants can answer rapidly. Second, the participants may be more apt to complete the evaluation because they can answer rapidly. Third, because answers are simple and direct the data can be easily analyzed.

The disadvantages can be summarized in two ways: the two choices may not be enough to fully explain the participant's attitudes and the questions may require extra care in writing to present clear questions and alternatives.

"Many choice" questions ask a participant to respond to a specific area through the use of many choices of answers.

The following questions are examples.

> How well were the seminar objectives met? (Circle One)
> Low 1 2 3 4 5 High

> How well was the course content organized? (Circle One)
> Low 1 2 3 4 5 High

There are three basic advantages. The data is easily analyzed as the choices are standardized. The participant can answer rapidly and the total numbers are easily averaged for a mean score.

The disadvantages fall into three categories: participant response, discrimination standards and scoring patterns. Participant response refers to the thought that goes into the circled response to the question. Circling a number doesn't mean a participant "thought" about the question. A well-thought-out circle looks much the same as a "no" thought circle. Discrimination standards refer to the discriminating ability a participant must have to discriminate between 5-7 choices. What is the difference between circling a 2 or a 3. What is the basis for scoring a 5, a 4, etc.? Scoring patterns refer to the tendency participants have to choose from the middle of the list in a many choice question.

For best evaluation results, a combination of questions may be the alternative. The "two choice" question combined with the open-ended question asks the participant to respond to a specific area and also allows the participant to express his/her thinking. The following format is an example:

> Did the workshop leader speak clearly and distinctly?
> Yes___No___
> If no, please explain________________________________
> ____

In the above question the "no" response from a participant needs to be explained. A "no" response without further feedback does little to explain the participant's thinking. A recent evaluation form was returned this way:

> Did the leader speak clearly and distinctly? Yes___No ✓
> If no, explain: I am hard of hearing.

The "yes" response to the above question is the expected response for two reasons. First, it is assumed a trainer would have the competency to speak clearly. Second, the trainer is fulfilling his/her

Rights and Responsibilities as set forth at the beginning of the workshop.

The "no" response takes effort from the participant thereby decreasing the effect of those participants who rate randomly. The "If no, explain" forces the participant to identify the lack or conflict in the workshop. The thoughtful answer may now be useful evaluation data; and, by allowing space for criticism, the questions offset the tendency of some participants to only praise.

Can you determine what is "wrong" with the following evaluation questions? The following questions will give you an opportunity to test your understanding of effective evaluation questions.

Read through each question and determine whether or not the questions are valid for a post-participant evaluation. Explain your reasoning. If a question "does not work" develop a new question that reveals information about the topic.

1. Is the course content what you expected?________________

 ____

2. Was the teaching: Excellent_________Good_________ Mediocre_________ Poor _________ ?

 ____

 ____

3. What would you suggest to improve this course?

 ____

 ____

 ____

4. Will the information presented be useful in your work?

 _______very useful _______useful _______a little useful
 _______not at all useful

 ____

 ____

5. On a scale of 1-5 with 5 as the highest, rate the following:

   This program was worth the cost_________
   This program was worth the time_________

   ____

   ____

6. Rate this program as to how well it will help you on the job.

   Excellent______ Good______ Fair______ Poor______

   ____

   ____

7. Did the instructor use the audio visual aids appropriately?

   Excellent______ Good______ Fair______ Poor______

   ____

   ____

8. Did this course meet your expectations as to what was advertised?
   Excellent______ Good______ Fair______ Poor______

   ____

   ____

9. What information did you expect to receive that you didn't get?______________________________________

   ____

   ____

10. What are you going to change when you get back to your job as a result of this workshop?

11. Using a scale of 1-7, with 1 as the lowest rating and 7 as the highest, rate the factual information presented.

12. The content of this program was pertinent to my personal needs and interests.

    Highest 5 4 3 2 1 Lowest

13. The course content concentrated on the important facts.

    Highest 5 4 3 2 1 Lowest

14. This information was new and interesting for me.

    Highest 5 4 3 2 1 Lowest

15. What information will be most useful on the job?__________

____

____

____

____

____

16. What information will be least useful on the job?__________

____

____

____

____

____

Bibliography

American Psychological Association. *Standards for Education and Psychological Tests* (rev. ed.). Washington, D.C.: American Psychological Association, 1974.

Chabotar, Kent J. and Lad, Lawrence J., "Research Designs: What Is the Best for You," adapted from *Evaluation Guidelines for Training Programs*, Midwest Intergovernmental Training Committee, U.S. Civil Service Commission.

Coker, Homer and Medley, Donald and Soar, Robert, *How Valid Are Expert Opinions About Effective Teaching?* Phi Delta Kappan, October 1980.

Coulson, J.E., and Cogswell, J. F., 1966, "Effects of individualized instruction and testing." *Journal of Educational Measurement.* 2: 59-64, 1966.

Darlington, Richard B., "Some techniques for maximizing a test's validity when the criticism variable is unobserved." *Journal of Educational Measurement*. 7:1-14,1970.

Ebel, R. L., *Essentials of Educational Measurement.* Englewood Cliffs, N.J.: Prentice-Hall, 1972.

Elsbree, Asia Rial and Howe, Christine, "An Evaluation of Training in Three Acts," *Training and Development Journal*, July, August, September, 1977.

Henrysson, S., "Gathering, analyzing and using data on test items." In R. L. Thorndike (ed.) *Educational Measurement.* Washington: American Council on Education, 1971.

Hoyer, Mary L., *An Evaluation of an Organizational Development and Training Effort in Management Communications Conducted at Fort Belvoir,* U.S. Office of Personnel Management, March, 1979.

Stufflebeam, D. L., "The use of experimental design in educational evaluation." *Journal of Educational Measurement*. 8:267-274, 1971.

Biography of the Author

Sandra Merwin

Sandra has written over 300 training programs, numerous magazine articles, and authored several books. In 1982 she received her brown belt in karate and wrote *Safe in the Streets - Don't be a Victim*, a book which explains how to stop crime from happening to you. In 1987 Sandra co-authored *The Mysteries of Motivation.* She was a co-author of the monograph, *Improving Human Resource Development Through Measurement*, which was published by the University of Minnesota Research Center and The American Society for Training and Development (ASTD) Research Center. In 1991 she wrote *Real Self: The Inner Journey of Courage* and in 1992 she authored *Figuring Kids Out: A Guide for Understanding Children.*

She is a past president of the Southern Minnesota Chapter of ASTD, has presented at five National ASTD conferences and was recognized as a Role Expert in Evaluation for National ASTD. In 1985 she received the ASTD/SMC Professional Excellence Award from Carlson Learning Company for her work in human behavior. In 1989 she received the ASTD Region VI Individual Chapter Service Award and her second Professional Excellence Award from the Southern Minnesota Chapter of ASTD for her contribution to the Human Resources Profession. Presently, Sandra serves as a National Advisor for Chapters of ASTD.

Robert W. Pike, CSP

Robert has developed and implemented training programs for business, industry, government and the professions since 1969. As president of Resources for Organizations, Inc. Creative Training Techniques International, Inc., and The Resources Group, Inc., Bob leads sessions over 150 days per year covering topics of leadership, attitudes, motivation, communication, decision-making, problem-solving, personal and organizational effectiveness, conflict management, team building and managerial productivity. More than 50,000 trainers have attended the Creative Training Techniques® workshop. As a consultant Bob has worked with such organizations as Pfizer, Upjohn, Caesars Boardwalk Regency, Exhibitor Magazine, Hallmark Cards Inc. and IBM.

Over the years Bob has contributed to magazines like "Training", "The Personnel Administrator" and "The Self Development Journal." He is editor of the "Creative Training Techniques Newsletter" and is author of "The Creative Training Techniques Handbook", "Developing, Marketing and Promoting Successful Seminars and Workshops" and "Improving Managerial Productivity".

13 Questions to Ask *Before* You Bring Anyone In-House

An in-house program is an investment. You want to ensure high return. Here are 13 questions to ask before you ask anyone to train your trainers (or train anyone else!).

1. What kind of measurable results have other clients had from your training?
2. How much experience does this company have in training trainers?
3. Is this 100 percent of what the company does or just part of what it does?
4. How experienced are the trainers who will work with our people?
5. How experienced are your trainers in maximizing training transfer to the job?
6. Is the program tailored to my needs, or is it the same content as the public program?
7. Why is an in-house program to our advantage?
8. Is team-building a by-product of the seminar?
9. Is there immediate application of new skills during the training session?
10. What kinds of resource and reference materials do we get?
11. What type of pre-course preparation or post-course follow-up do you do?
12. How are our participants recognized for their achievements?
13. Will you teach my trainers how to get participant buy-in, even from the difficult participant?

Advantages of a Customized, In-House Program with Creative Training Techniques™ International, Inc.

Customized in-house programs provide your organization with training tailored to your specific needs. Our unique participant-centered teaching style is a revolutionary new training approach that is far more effective than traditional lecture-based training. This training approach has been adapted by a wide range of industries including healthcare, finance, communications, government, and non-profit agencies. Our clients include American Express, AT&T, Hewlett-Packard, 3M, U.S. Healthcare, and Tonka Corporation. We are eager to learn about your training needs and discuss how we can provide solutions. Please give us a call so we can help your company create a more vital and effective workforce.